DBT Skill-Buil[ding Workbook]

Help Kids to Deal with St[ress, A...] Control E[motions]

By

W. Mumtaz

About the Author

W. Mumtaz is a child psychologist. She is an expert in cognitive-behavioral therapy (CBT) to treat OCD and associated anxiety disorders in children and teenagers. In CBT therapy for anxiety disorders, W. Mumtaz has offered direct patient care and taught child and adolescent therapists and psychologists. She is currently working in a public hospital with special needs children. She has a keen interest in screen-free parenting and child development. She designs age-appropriate activities for developmental milestones. She is experienced in assessing and devising intervention plans for children's behavioral problems. She is a key public voice teaching children and parents about the fear at the base of anxiety and how it may properly be handled. She is a passionate supporter of the mental health of children and young people.

Contents

Introduction

If your child has trouble coping with their feelings, they may have trouble focusing or following the school standards. They may have difficulty getting along with others, especially their colleagues and teachers.

You might be wondering when your child's conduct will improve.

Your child may lash out at you, particularly if you try to enforce healthy norms and boundaries. They could throw tantrums and meltdowns when you ask them to finish their schoolwork or brush their teeth. It is possible that every day feels like a war.

Perhaps you have already sought help, and your kid has been identified with ADHD, anxiety, etc. You may have tried every therapy and parenting style available, but none has shown effectiveness. It is possible that your youngster still feels lonely, vulnerable, and lost.

BUT...

Do you think you could assist your child in recognizing the value of their sensitivity while simultaneously providing them with the tools they need to navigate their environment?

AND...

Do you want to develop different parenting techniques to help your child cope with challenging emotions, connect with others, and move forward with joy, confidence, and peace?

YES!

Dialectical behavior therapy (DBT) is a type of cognitive-behavioral therapy (CBT) that has been modified.

DBT was created to treat bipolar disorder (BPD), but it has now been used to treat various other mental illnesses. It can assist individuals who have a problem controlling their emotions or engage in self-destructive behavior. Post-traumatic stress disorder (PTSD) is sometimes treated with this form of therapy.

DBT has evolved into an evidence-based psychotherapy strategy that can be used to treat various issues. Group therapy, in which patients are taught behavioral skills in a group environment, is one scenario where DBT is commonly employed.

Individual therapy with a trained professional applies a patient's newly acquired behavioral skills to their specific life issues. Patients can phone their therapist during sessions to get advice on dealing with a challenging circumstance they are now facing.

In DBT, the patient and therapist work together to reconcile the seeming tension between self-acceptance and transformation to help the person in therapy make good changes. Offering validation is a part of this process, making people more ready to collaborate and less likely to be distressed by the prospect of change.

In practice, the therapist confirms that a person's behaviors "make sense" in the context of their life observations without actually agreeing that these are the best ways to solve an issue. Although the structure and aims of each therapeutic environment differ, these DBT features can be accompanied by additional skills training, private psychotherapy, and telephone coaching.

Acceptance and Change: You'll discover techniques for accepting and tolerating your life situation, feelings, and yourself. You will also gain skills that will assist you in making positive adjustments in your conduct and relationships with others.

Behaviors: You'll learn to identify problems and detrimental behavior patterns, then replace them with healthier and more productive ones.

Cognitive: You'll concentrate on modifying ineffective or harmful attitudes and beliefs.

Collaboration: You'll learn how to communicate and collaborate as a group successfully.

Skill sets: You'll gain new talents by learning new skills.

Encourage: You'll be urged to recognize and enhance your good strengths and attributes.

People can discover efficient strategies to control and express powerful emotions with this approach to treatment since it can help them improve their coping abilities. According to researchers, DBT is also beneficial regardless of a person's age, gender, gender identification, sexual preference, or race/ethnicity.

"DBT necessitates a large time commitment".

People are required to do "homework" in addition to regular treatment sessions to work on skills beyond the individual, groups, and telephone counseling sessions. This could be a problem for persons who have difficulties keeping up with these tasks regularly. For some people, practicing some of the abilities can be difficult. People explore traumatic events and emotional distress at various stages of treatment, which can be painful.

DBT teaches children how to connect to others in a more positive way. DBT teaches students how to recognize when they are coping with a situation in an unhelpful way. It also equips patients with the tools to effectively manage their difficulties and maintain healthy habits such as eating properly, getting

9

adequate rest, taking their medications, and abstaining from drugs. Keep reading and I will tell you how DBT can help your kids with different mental health issues.

A Note for Grownups

You're undoubtedly curious about DBT and whether it's right for you and your child. We hope that this book will answer your questions regarding DBT and inspire you to heal.

Bringing up children is a difficult task. It might be difficult to know whether a youngster requires assistance or simply goes through a developmental phase. You do not have to tackle the hardships of child-rearing alone as a parent; we are here to assist.

Children, like adults, have good days and bad days. We expect a youngster to become impatient, angry, or unhappy from time to time. On the other hand, some youngsters are prone to powerful emotions and maybe angry or irritable practically every day of the week. A child who is frequently overwhelmed by emotions may have frequent outbursts of anger or act rashly.

If your kid has frequent tantrums, you may be asking how to cope with an angry child and whether or not child stress management therapy works.

How do you recognize when a child's behavior necessitates the intervention of a professional?

You are not alone if you don't know where to start or what to do. Coping with difficult behaviors and emotions is difficult for both parents and children, but there is hope — regardless of the origin of the behavior.

Consider Dialectical Behavior Treatment for children. The goal of DBT is to assist parents in supporting their children in gaining effective coping skills. Although DBT is a comparatively recent treatment approach for children, it has proven beneficial. Children acquire DBT coping strategies with powerful emotions and appreciate their time with family and friends and all the stuff that makes them happy.

Children do not have the potential to fully benefit from DBT independently, and they need their parents' help to harvest the most long-term advantages of DBT treatment. DBT's parent component prepares parents to take over as their child's counselor, once treatment is completed. This ongoing support is essential for a child's success with DBT coping strategies.

Parents do not need to be concerned; they will receive all necessary information throughout their child's treatment. Parents, for example, will discover how to demonstrate skills, provide a supportive environment, and assist their child in practicing DBT skills daily. The parent element of DBT tries to enhance the child-parent relationship as well.

DBT is a highly effective technique for children that focuses on assisting your child in understanding their unique role in the world. Your child can be himself in a safe, friendly environment.

> Being sensitive does not necessarily imply that something is wrong. It is just a different way of looking at things.

Your child will be welcomed into an environment tailored to meet their needs. They will learn how to adjust their actions to simplify life through activities centered on acceptability and positive reward rather than punishment. This is a type of family and children counseling. Your active participation as a parent is critical to your child's long-term development.

A Message for Kids

Hey kids! I have a story for you. Let's read out loud.

Rachel's childhood was not easy. Her mother's severe sickness placed her in the hospital for a long when she was a child. She suffered extreme anxiety as a child and struggled to make friends at school. She eventually developed an eating disorder and began self-harming at thirteen. She said, "I had what you'd call a breakdown when I was 15. I was out of school for the majority of the year." Rachel had been in treatment for quite some time, but it had primarily consisted of unstructured conversation therapy and medication. She was admitted to an adolescent ward at a hospital she described as horrific and terrible when she began to have suicidal thoughts. "Another patient assaulted me, and no one did anything". Rachel said that she left the session sadder.

However, she then switched to a DBT-trained therapist. Thanks to the DBT therapy techniques, she was enrolled in a 28-day DBT "activity camp" for kids that included an eating disorders program. "For 28 days, we learned and practiced DBT every day," she recalls. Rachel is doing extremely well just after a year. She finds some of the strategies she learned in DBT to be more useful than others, so she concentrates her efforts there. "The key ones for me are anxiety tolerance, concentration, and emotional regulation abilities," she explains. "I don't get into fights with individuals or even my parents, so interpersonal effectiveness abilities are very useful to me."

Rachel relies significantly on diary cards—daily diaries that document her moods and feelings, what triggers them, and how she reacts to them both positively and negatively—and a set of skills she has developed to deal with unpleasant emotions. She has a total of 19 diaries so far. She also does a lot of breathing exercises to get herself in the right frame of mind.

"DBT saved her life," Rachel's father said.

On the other side, Rachel says that it isn't quite that straightforward.

"DBT and its activities saved my life".

Chapter 1: Basics of DBT Therapy

Dr. Marsha Linehan and collaborators created DBT in the late 1980s after discovering that Cognitive-Behavioral Therapy (CBT) alone did not function as effectively as expected in individuals with bipolar disorder. Dr. Linehan and her team tweaked approaches and created a treatment to match these people's specific needs. Interpersonal effectiveness, mindfulness, distress tolerance, and emotion regulation are the four emotional and psychological function modules that DBT works on. In both individual and group treatment, skill development in these four components is traditionally done systematically and gradually. DBT, like other types of CBT, concentrates on the client's day-to-day functioning and includes skill teaching and encouragement of skill practice outside of treatment sessions.

1.1 DBT Interpersonal Effectiveness Module

Interpersonal effectiveness enables you to be more forceful in a relationship (for example, by expressing your wants and saying "no") while maintaining a happy and healthy relationship. You will improve your listening and communication skills and your ability to deal with difficult individuals and respect yourself and others.

DBT teaches kids interpersonal skills that will help them acquire what they desire while sustaining relationships with their peers, family, and others. Children learn to express themselves directly and how to ask for what they want while remaining forceful, respectful, and fair.

1.2 Distress Tolerance Module

Skills in distress tolerance assist you in accepting yourself and your current circumstances. DBT offers a variety of crisis-handling methods, including:

- Distraction
- Making things better
- Self-soothing
- Consider the advantages and disadvantages of not accepting distress.

Distress tolerance tactics help you prepare for strong emotions and equip you to deal with them more positively in the long run.

Distress tolerance skills assist youngsters in navigating challenging situations without exacerbating the problem. Dealing with reality rather than fighting to handle stress is the key to stress tolerance. To get through a difficult situation, children will learn to control their emotions and conduct.

A therapist might, for example, urge a kid to try diversions like watching a movie to help him get through a difficult time. A therapist might suggest using self-soothing tactics like listening to soothing music or taking a warm bath to get through a crisis. Parents will discover unique techniques to help their child cope with a hard situation throughout DBT treatment tailored to their child's needs.

1.3 Emotion Regulation Module

Emotion control allows you to deal with strong emotions more effectively. The techniques you learn will assist you in recognizing, naming, and altering your emotions. It minimizes your emotional sensitivity and enables you to have more pleasant emotional experiences when you notice and manage severe negative feelings (such as anger).

Emotion management abilities can assist a youngster in reducing the pain associated with strong emotions. DBT helps children be aware of their feelings and see them like a wave. DBT's purpose is not to get rid of feelings but to help a kid "surf" an emotional wave to reduce pain and vulnerability.

DBT also stresses physical wellness, learning to let go of worry, making objectives, and generating happy emotions. Children learn that negativity is not their feelings and that they do not have to do what their emotions urge them to do throughout DBT.

1.4 Mindfulness Module

The mindfulness skill is at the heart of DBT.

The strengthening of relaxation techniques is a key benefit of DBT. Mindfulness allows kids to "live in the moment" by focusing on the present. This allows them to pay attention to what's going on inside them (thoughts, feelings, sensations, and impulses) while also utilizing the senses to tune in to what's going on around them (what they are seeing, hearing, sensing, and touching) in a nonjudgmental way.

When you are dealing with emotional discomfort, mindfulness techniques can make you slow down and concentrate on adopting appropriate coping strategies. The technique can also assist you in remaining calm and avoiding negative thinking and impulsive actions.

Children will learn and practice mindfulness strategies to be aware of their thoughts and feelings in the present moment during individual activity sessions of the book.

The concept of three states of consciousness – the emotional mind, the logical mind, and the wise mind – is one of the principles employed in DBT. The smart mind embodies a delicate mix of emotions and facts. Children will learn "what" and "how" skills to help them activate their wise minds. What skills do you need to observe and describe what the youngster is going through? How skills educate a youngster on responding to the realities of a situation and achieving goals by analyzing data etc.

1.5 DBT Success Stories

Want to listen more stories? I have some other stories of kids who are living their life to the fullest after DBT treatment.

Story-I

For a student who tried her hardest to portray herself as a "tough girl," self-validation was a life-changing experience. She often lashed out at the individuals she cared about instead of communicating her emotions; she would yell, fight, and push people away. She seldom cried, and when she did, you could see the agony and embarrassment on her face as she cried or felt emotion, and then she would calm down.

During the self-validation activity of DBT sessions, she told herself, "It's acceptable that I'm unhappy right now. It's fine that I'm crying as a result of what occurred. This is how anyone in my situation would feel". She transformed mentally and behaviorally as she accepted that it was okay to feel emotions. She was able to see things from other people's points of view, be more understanding of herself and people, and work through difficult situations without causing harm to her relationships.

Story-II

With their daughter, Jia's parents recently told this story of DBT sessions. They said that Jia had decided not to study for a test, and as a result, she had failed it. She was disappointed and unhappy that she did not receive a higher grade. We were worried and angry. We were afraid of her mental health. One day, someone told us to visit a nearby therapist. We were calm and understanding toward Jia after attending 3 DBT sessions arranged for parents. We did not validate her bad study practices, but we affirmed her feelings by saying, "We understand that you're disappointed with your grade. That is extremely difficult. We are hoping you'll study for your next exam". We successfully communicated to Jia that we recognized her feelings without validating her actions while encouraging her to improve.

Story-III

Let's listen this story in Patrick's words.

My name is Patrick. For the past 6 or 7 months, I've been attending DBT sessions at San Diego. DBT appears to be assisting me in a variety of ways. Before DBT, I didn't know how to deal with situations healthily. DBT has provided me with some beneficial abilities. I have learned to recognize it when I am upset, anxious, or depressed. I've been trying certain techniques until my body relaxes and my hands loosen up. I'm not obligated to act on my emotions straight away. I can leave the matter on the back burner for a time and return to it when I am calmer. I've also discovered that I have choices. When I'm intimidated or ignored, I choose how I respond. I've discovered that doing the "opposite action" to how I want to react can make things go more smoothly. I've discovered that my mind can only concentrate on one task at a time. I strive to focus entirely and work through the situation at hand. I've learned to love myself, and I'm growing in my acceptance of others. I still have to work on being nonjudgmental, but I'm becoming better at it.

Mindfulness appeals to me since it has caused me to reflect more on myself and my environment. Now that I can see the larger picture, it's easier for me to make smarter judgments that won't lead to further problems. I have a hard time going to groups, but I try to force myself to go nonetheless. I am occasionally capable of learning from other people's experiences and stories. When the leaders present the skills, I try to think about how that skill would benefit me. I used to be quite hesitant to ask inquiries. DBT has taught me how to ask and receive answers to the questions on my mind. Then I won't have to be concerned or concerned about anything. DBT has given me the confidence to ask questions, and the responses have frequently been better than my expectations. I'm interested in learning more about DBT. I intend to use what I've learned while also learning new abilities. I intend to add more tools to my toolbox because one can never have too many. Even if I have to spend a lot of time on the bus to get to San Diego, I believe I will return for DBT groups and sessions with my counselor after I leave.

Chapter 2: Getting Started with DBT: Interpersonal Effectiveness

A closer relationship can be compared to a tall, lush tree. A robust root system is required to feed and support a tree. The tree gets larger, tougher, and more developed as the roots grow, and they may even bear fruit! Your interpersonal ties, like the tree, have roots. Good roots are necessary for the growth of a healthy relationship. DBT (Dialectical Behavioral Therapy) teaches specialized strategies for establishing deep roots and maintaining healthy relationships.

These abilities are crucial because how we communicate with others affects the quality of our relations and how our interactions turn out. DBT clients are given strategies to help them approach discussions more thoughtfully and deliberately rather than behaving and reacting quickly due to stress or powerful emotions to interact more effectively. The capacity to ask for things and, when necessary, saying no to requests are two crucial components of interpersonal competence. In this chapter, I am going to teach you some effective strategies and activities so that you can know yourself better.

Goal Sheet

Why? A simple goals sheet can be a big thing when dealing with parents of young children. This worksheet is straightforward and to the point. First, make a list of your weekly objectives. This could be a duty ("I'll clean my bedroom every day") or a way to avoid undesired behavior ("When I'm frustrated, I'll practice my anger management skills").

Note for Kids: Take a little time in the session, in addition to setting down an everyday aim, to describe exactly how it works. Use caution when setting broad goals, such as "I would be good the whole day." What is "good" to a parent and what is "good" to a child are likely to be very different, and conflicts after the fact can be a genuine issue.

Note for Parents: It will be the parents' responsibility to keep track of their child's progress toward their goal each night and to deliver an appropriate reward after a set number of completions. It is good for parents to talk about why their children met or missed their daily objectives.

My goal for this week is to:

Monday	Tuesday	Wednesday	Thursday	Friday	Saturday	Sunday

22

Where Do I Feel?

Note for Parents: Use art to help kids name, identify, and acknowledge their emotions and the body sensations that go along with them. Ask your kids to pick a color to represent each emotion, then draw a cartoon as given below and color in the area of their body where they feel it. Children may, for example, color fists red to signify rage. Happiness could be described as a yellow light.

Allowing your kids to be creative with this art therapy project is a great approach to get youngsters talking about their emotions. We recommend devoting a little more time talking about specific body experiences that come with emotions. What does rage feel like in your fist, for example? Is it painful, or does it make you feel good? Improving this type of insight will assist children in being more aware of their emotions on critical occasions.

Where Do I Feel?

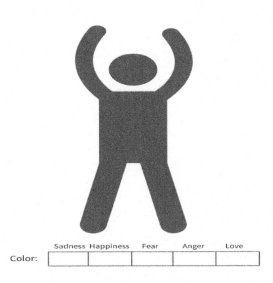

	Sadness	Happiness	Fear	Anger	Love
Color:					

Personal Identity Wheel

Note for Parents: In the empty boxes on the wheel, ask kids to write down their;

- Favorite Music
- Birth Order
- Number of Siblings
- Personal Motto
- Favorite Color
- One Skill you are Proud of
- Favorite Movie
- Favorite Food
- Favorite Hobby
- Favorite Book

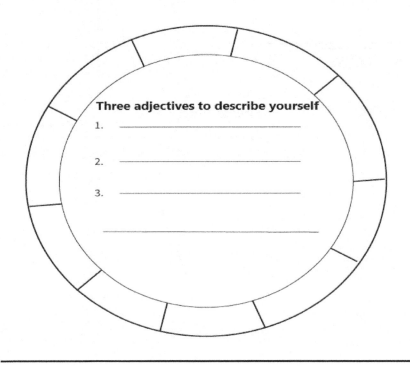

Three adjectives to describe yourself

1. _____

2. _____

3. _____

_____

My Strengths and Qualities

Note for Parents: These strengths and qualities worksheets will help your kids to identify the good and bad in them. They will be able to accept their flaws and appreciate their uniqueness. Ask kids to write the things that come to their minds after listening to these questions.

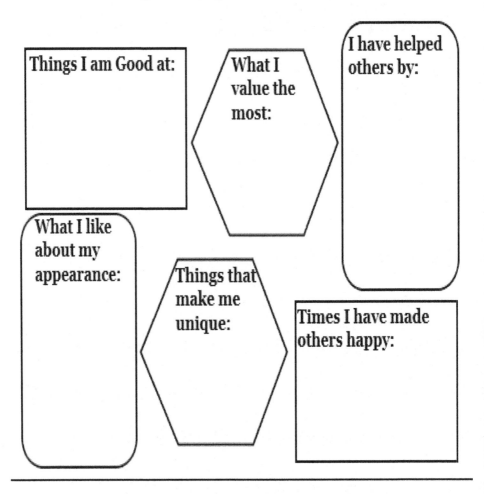

Things I am Good at:

What I value the most:

I have helped others by:

What I like about my appearance:

Things that make me unique:

Times I have made others happy:

My Weaknesses

Note for Parents: Youngsters need to accept their weaknesses. Kids mostly compare themselves with their colleagues and friends. Everyone is born different with different qualities and weaknesses. With this activity, help your kids to identify their weaknesses.

My Top Ten Weaknesses

1. _____   6. _____

2. _____   7. _____

3. _____   8. _____

4. _____   9. _____

5. _____   10. _____

One of my weaknesses that is now my strength:

One weakness I would like to make my strength is:

My Priorities

Note for Parents: Does your kid find it difficult to complete tasks because they feel tired and the day feels busy and hectic? Isn't there never enough opportunity in the day to get everything done?

Your kid probably doesn't have a clear sense of priorities, if you silently answered yes in your brain. It's tricky for kids to handle time and achieve goals as they don't have clear priorities. They may be overburdening themselves by attempting to shoulder too many homework tasks. Our priorities typically determine our freedom to move forward and achieve our objectives. Your kid will be able to make good and faster selections that will govern their life choices once they have established priorities.

If you are having trouble defining your kids' top life priorities, I have put together a quick activity to help you figure it out. Plus, I will show you how to make the same quick and easy flowchart I use to establish my priorities.

DEFINE YOUR PRIORITIES

I feel happiest when:

I feel stressed-out when:

My 3 Priority Things that I want in my life:

3 things that I want less in my life:

MAKING SPACE IN MY LIFE FOR WHAT MATTERS

Today, I will	This Week, I will	This month, I will

I will stay accountable by:

I will next review my priorities on:

Sabotage Exercise

When it applies to early language development, sabotage is not always negative. It is a fantastic method to get your child to start a conversation. You are not putting your child up for failure by sabotaging the environment. It truly refers to creating a play situation or activity where your youngster will require your assistance. Here are three methods to utilize sabotage in your own home:

Puzzles

Many children like solving puzzles. Set up parts that are just out of reach of your youngster so that they must ask for help and make a comment about anything being wrong. You can even hide one component so that one piece remains missing when the youngster has completed the puzzle. This may encourage your child to make a statement or ask for help.

Basketball

Do you have a ball and hoop in your house? To urge your child to speak, use sabotage while learning the game. Place the ball on a high shelf and wait for them to ask for it. Some toy hoops have adjustable heights, so you can raise and lower them as needed. When you adjust the height, see if your child comments on how tall or short it is and requests it to be raised or lowered.

Play-Doh

You can use Play-Doh to encourage your kid to request, comment, label, and gesture on the spur of the moment. You can put Play-Doh in a clear container so that they have to ask for it if they see it and want to use it. Put one or more Play-Doh tools inside a box or carton that cannot be opened without support to elicit spontaneous language.

Remember to have fun with environmental sabotage! During these activities, your child should not become frustrated or upset. Instead, make the activities lively, and if your youngster is not speaking, you can present instances and models to urge them to mimic your statements and avoid frustration!

Accept the Reality Worksheet

Note for Parents: Accepting life on its terms rather than opposing what you cannot alter is what radical acceptance is all about. This is how it works. Assume you are in line for a job. You were qualified for the position, nailed every meeting, and the recruiter gave you every reason to feel you were a lock for the job. Then you came to know that a different candidate received the position at the last minute.

Perhaps it was unjust, or perhaps the applicant was more qualified, but you are dissatisfied and frustrated in either case. The same happens with kids. Even the smallest thing can make them disappoint. They are more likely to distract from reality as compared to adults. Accepting that you have no power in some life situations is the first step toward radical acceptance. Everyone, including children, can practice true radical acceptance with this activity. Help kids to fill out this activity.

Reality Acceptance

What's the situation?

What led up to the situation?

Which things you could control?

How did you react to the situation?

What is the reality?

Feelings Hopscotch

Note for Kids: It is a type of feelings block game. You need to write your upsetting feelings in the blocks and then fill the blocks with your favorite colors. You can also draw patterns and shapes to make it a good look feeling.

Feeling Hopscotch

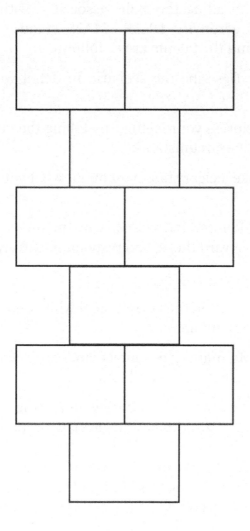

DEAR MAN

Acronyms are used in dialectical behavior therapy to assist individuals in recalling the skills associated with each type of efficacy. The acronym DEAR MAN stands for objective effectiveness, and the talents are as follows:

D – Describe: Describe the scenario in detail without passing judgment.

E - Express: Express your feelings by telling the other party how you feel about the circumstance.

A - Assert: Make a clear statement about what you want or don't want.

R - Reinforce: Remind individuals why the intended outcome is desirable, and reward those who respond positively.

M - Mindful: Focus on the current goal while remaining mindful and present at the moment.

A - Appear: Maintain eye contact and project confidence by adopting a confident stance and tone.

N - Negotiate: Be open to negotiating and giving to receive while considering that both sides have legitimate needs and feelings.

**Help kids to remember this skill and make them apply these thoughts in their everyday life.

GIVE and FAST

Moving on to the effectiveness of relationships, the next DBT skill is GIVE:

G - Gentle: Contact the other person in a non-threatening and gentle way, avoiding attacks and harsh words.

I - Interested: Show that you are interested in paying attention to what the other person is saying and not interrupting them.

V – Validate: Accept and recognize the other person's wishes, feelings, and ideas.

E — Easy: Maintain a relaxed demeanor by smiling and speaking in a light, amusing tone.

Finally, FAST stands for the DBT acronym for consciousness effectiveness:

F - Fair: To avoid hatred on both sides, be fair to oneself and others.

A - Apologize: Apologize less frequently and take responsibility only when necessary.

S - Stick: Don't compromise your integrity to achieve a goal.

T - Sincere: Be sincere and resist exaggerating or appearing helpless to influence others.

ACCEPTS

We can use a variety of tactics to divert ourselves. The term ACCEPTS is another DBT skill.

A - Activities: Watch an episode of your favorite series, go for a stroll or exercise, play computer games, clean a room or area in your home, spend time with a friend or family, read a book, or finish a puzzle.

C – Connect: Volunteering is a great way to give back to the community. Assist a family member or friend with a task. Donate any stuff you no longer need or simply do something pleasant for someone else, such as encouraging them or hugging them.

C - Contrasts: Consider how you feel now against how you felt in the past. Consider how fortunate you are, and consider how many other people worldwide are coping with the same problem.

E - Emotions: Read a book that will make you feel something. Watch a heartfelt film. Listen to a song or album that has a lot of power. It could be any number of emotions. Listen to soothing music or watch a scary or comic film.

P - Pushing away: Put whatever is bothering you to the side for a bit. For a time, ignore the issue. Refuse to think about or block out anxious memories or images from your mind.

T – Thoughts: Add up something, whether the number of petals in a pot or counting to ten. In your head, repeat the lyrics of your favorite song, or watch or read thought-provoking stuff.

S – Sensations: Take a deep breath and squeeze that stress ball. Shower, either hot or cold. Alternatively, turn up the volume on your music.

Chapter 2: Distress Tolerance: Dealing with Stress and Anxiety

Sitting in traffic congestion, realizing you are out of espresso as you go to make your cup of coffee, or having a low car battery without accessibility to a charger are all unpleasant scenarios. We all experience more serious sorrow and pain at points in our lives, such as the loss of a friend, the loss of a spouse, or the loss of a job. Some people, particularly those with Borderline Personality Disorder (BPD), are more sensitive to the pain and suffering of these situations than others. Individuals may experience an intense sense of pain that appears to come from within and is unrelated to what is happening around them.

Dialectical Behavior Therapy (DBT) includes a module called Distress Tolerance, which teaches various skills. These talents are often referred to as "crisis survival skills because they assist a person in navigating a (real or perceived) crisis,"

Whether perceived or real, emotional tension is difficult to manage, especially for those who have experienced trauma. When people feel powerless and out of control during a disaster, this inability may worsen. Distress tolerance refers to a person's ability to cope with an emotional event without being overwhelmed.

Every one of us will face a crisis at some point in our life. A breakup, a death, or a layoff are major crises. These crises can be minor, such as traffic, a long line at the check-out counter, or not knowing what to dress that day. DBT distress tolerance abilities assist you in achieving a more controllable emotional state to survive a crisis.

A person's distress tolerance skills enable them to endure an immediate emotional meltdown without exacerbating it. They also assist people in accepting the reality of the circumstance when they feel powerless to change the issue.

Distress tolerance skills can assist kids in coping with their emotions when they are unsure of what they want or require at the time.

Distress tolerance is a skill that can assist a kid in reducing the intensity of emotional discomfort. Other DBT coping skills, such as regulating emotions, meditation, and interpersonal skills, are also useful. Here I have some activities for kids to deal with anxiety.

Name My Anxiety

What are some things your anxiety says to you?

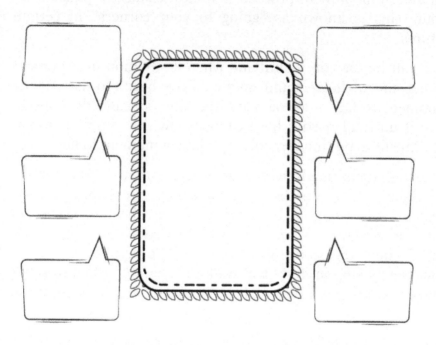

What are some things you can start saying back?

41

Moment to Pause

Since DBT is about identifying how your body reacts to stress and establishing internal systems to notice and re-route tension or irritation in healthy ways, pausing is a crucial DBT skill.

Allowing your child to take a breath, step back from a situation, and determine how to proceed is what a chance of pause is all about. This is known as "going to your corners" in certain cultures.

This skill focuses on identifying when a situation or argument has become too heated, and emotions have begun to rise. Taking a moment to halt is recognizing the situation and deciding to leave it until all parties have calmed down. A simple concept, but difficult to put into practice, is taking a moment to halt.

By giving their children a code word, parents can use this technique to educate them on managing stress and anxiety. Consider this scenario: two siblings have a heated discussion that quickly devolves into a brawl when someone says, "Code red!" When the code word is used, everyone agrees to immediately stop arguing and walk to separate rooms to settle down for a minute, allowing the siblings to step back from the issue.

To learn and practice something is challenging sometimes, but one of the most significant abilities you can teach your children as they grow up is the ability to take a moment to pause.

<u>Worry Exploration Worksheet</u>

Note for Parents: When people are worried, they often imagine the worst possible scenario. In actuality, these fears may never be realized. What may occur is not the same as what will occur. Kids are challenged to explore their worry vs. reality in the Worry Questions worksheet. They are urged to consider the most probable results for their worried-about circumstance through a sequence of questions rather than the worst-case scenarios. During DBT, this worksheet can be useful for questioning illogical ideas. Each question has been written keeping children in mind yet with enough depth for teens and adults.

What could happen vs. What Will happen

When you are anxious about something, it is too simple to imagine the worst-case scenario. In actuality, these fears may never be realized. What may occur is not the same as what will occur.

What is it about which you are concerned?

Instead of worrying about what might happen, think about what will happen. When your kids are worried, ask these questions:

What are some signs that your fear is unfounded?

What will most likely happen if your fear is not realized?

How will you deal with their fear if it comes true? Are you going to be okay in the end?

How has your worry altered as a result of answering these questions?

Worry Coping Cards

Note for Parents: Worry and rumination can be managed with the use of coping strategies. When employed regularly, these approaches can assist control long-term anxiety and provide a distraction from ruminating. Each anxiety coping card describes a different technique for dealing with worries, such as deep breathing, writing, or mindfulness. Each card contains a bright graphic on the front to help kids remember the method, and the backside has a kid-friendly explanation of each technique.

These coping cards are a good way to remember what your kids learned. Alternatively, incorporate the cards into a game scenario that your kids already enjoy. For instance, each time your kids take a turn in a game, ask them to choose a coping card and explain how they could use it to manage their anxiety. Try an expanded version of these cards and other stress activities for kids.

Worry Coping Cards

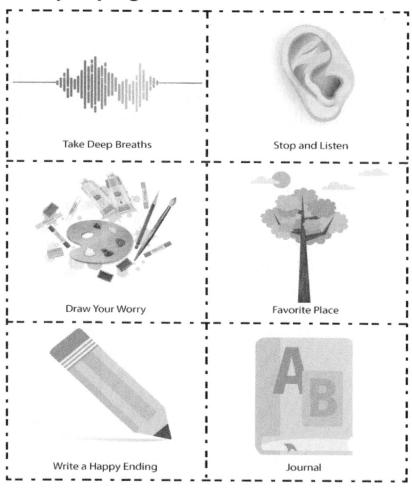

There are more ways to deal with your kids' anxiety. Follow the directions.

- **Take a moment to listen.**

Take a few moments to listen to the sounds surrounding you simply. What are the sounds you are hearing? Is it loud or soft?

Pay close attention to any unusual sounds you have never heard before.

- **Take a few deep breaths in and out.**

Inhale slowly and deeply via your nose, holding the air in your chest. Put your lips together again and pretend to blow through a straw when you are ready to let go of the air. Repeat this process twenty times.

- **Favorite Spot**

Consider a place where you feel at ease, and ease. It may be on a beach, in the woods, in your house, or somewhere else entirely. Consider how this place looks and sounds and how amazing you will feel once you are there.

- **Draw Your Anxiety**

Make a drawing of your concern or anxiety. Here are some suggestions:

1. How you appear when you are scared versus when you are relaxed.
2. What you can do to get rid of your worries.
3. An issue that you are concerned about.

- **Journal**

Write down your concerns. To begin, consider the following questions:

1. What are your main concerns?
2. When you are worried, what do you do?
3. When was the last time you were concerned about a similar issue?

- **Write a good ending for your story.**

When you are worried, you usually imagine things going wrong. Try writing about your concern, but end on a positive one. Write about how you solved an issue, relaxed, felt better, or dealt with your anxiety.

- **Consider What It Is**

When you are worried, you are usually thinking about the worst-case scenario. Instead, consider what truly occurs the majority of the time. Instead of thinking to yourself, "I am concerned and I'll miss my school bus," try thinking to yourself, "I've never missed my bus before."

- **Let's Talk About It**

One of the most effective strategies to control your sentiments is to talk about them. Tell a trusted person about your concerns, such as a parent, friend, teacher, or counselor. To begin, consider the following sentence:

"When _____," I think to myself.

- **Play Some Music**

Enjoying your favorite music can help you forget about your worries. Concentrate your attention on the song's instrumentation, lyrics, and singers.

- **Get to work!**

Being active is a great way to expend energy. Play a sport, ride your bike, dance, swim, walk, or run till you are exhausted.

- **Take up a new hobby.**

Do whatever hobby you think will help you forget about your worries. Play an instrument, paint, practice a new skill, play a game, or engage in any other activity that you find enjoyable.

My Fears Worksheet

Note for Parents: Using the My Fears anxiety worksheet, prompt youngsters to start a discussion about anxiety and fear. This worksheet will allow your kids to talk about their fears and anxieties, why they are significant, and how they can affect them. Children are instructed to write down their concerns, explain their thoughts about the worry, pinpoint where the feeling occurs in their bodies, and ultimately devise a strategy for dealing with dread in the future. The purpose of this worksheet is to introduce children to the concept of thoughts and feelings being linked and develop their awareness of their feelings by asking them to recognize how their bodies react to anxiousness.

What are some things that make you feel nervous or scared? _____

_____

_____

When you are nervous, you feel:_____

_____

How does your body feel when you are scared?

Color the areas where you feel nervousness.

What is in Your Heart?

Note for Kids: Write down different emotions in front of the colors. Make a pattern in the heart and color the blanks in the heart. In the end, observe how your heart is feeling and what made your heart in this situation.

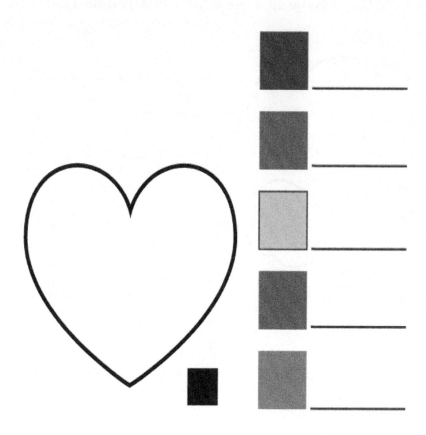

Anxiety vs. Truth

Note for Kids: You have 2 different shapes. Cloud shape is for your anxiety thought record and the other one is for the truth record. Consider a situation and write down your anxiety thoughts related to that event. When the event has passed, write the truth that was the opposite of your anxiety thought.

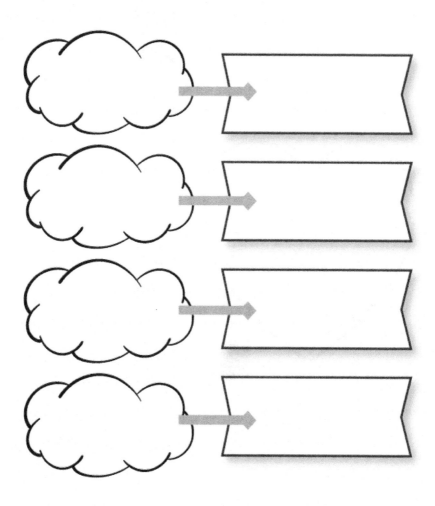

If I didn't Care

Note for Kids: It is a simple exercise to know the consequences. You just need to think of some circumstances and complete the sentences as if you didn't care for those things, what would happen?

If I didn't care

I would _____

I would not _____

I would listen to _____

I would try _____

I would _____

I would not _____

I would go _____

I would _____

I would say _____

I would start _____

I would _____

I would watch _____

I would stop _____

I Love Me

Note for Kids: Draw a heart with this heart tree each day. When feeling upset, draw smaller and when excited or happier, draw the big one.

I Love Me

Anxiety Steps

Note for Kids: These are some anxiety steps. You need to write down all the things that make you anxious and make you distracted from your life goals. Write the goals of your life in the center.

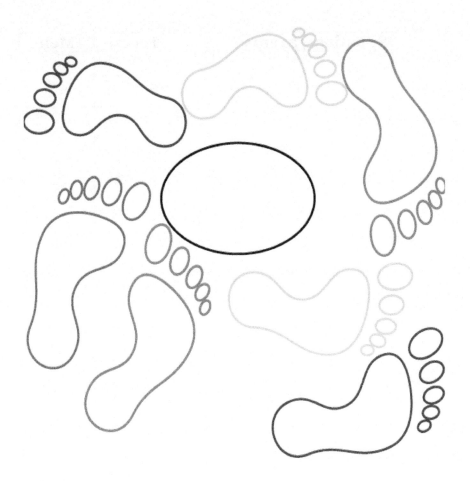

Freeze and Melt

Note for Kids: Here I have two options for you. You can either freeze or melt. Think of some life events and decide If you want to freeze at the moment or want to melt. (Freeze: to become strong, Melt: to become soft-hearted).

Situations/Events	Freeze	Melt

Chapter 3: Control your Kids' Anger

Is it possible for your kid's happiness to convert into anger?

Do your kids make snap decisions that they later come to regret?

Are you looking for ways to keep your kid's temper under control?

Dr. John analyses the emotion of rage and argues that anger has acquired a poor rap in modern culture. You will discover some important techniques from Dialectical Behavior Therapy to help your kids avoid anger from turning into wrath as part of the chapter.

What is Anger?

Note for Parents: Basic psychoeducation is usually the first step in managing anger in youngsters. Kids who haven't had much experience talking about sentiments may struggle to describe their feelings, recognize triggers, and connect the implications of their anger to the repercussions they have experienced. As a result, ample time should be spent reviewing these themes before diving into anger control techniques. This anger management exercise worksheet describes and normalizes anger using kid-friendly language. The exercises aim to help kids consider how they act differently when they are angry, understand their causes, and then come up with alternative ways to respond when they are furious.

Draw a picture of what you look like when you are angry

What's something you say when you are angry?

List some things that make you angry:

1. _____

2. _____

3. _____

4. _____

5. _____

Some healthy things to do when you feel angry:

Take deep breaths.
Draw your anger.
Do jumping jacks.
Write about your anger.
Count to 100.
Talk to someone.
Walk away.
Play outside.
Squeeze a stress ball.
Practice a hobby.
Listen to music.

How Does Anger Feel?

Note for Parents: This is a fun and understanding exercise for kids. Ask kids to note down all the things they feel while experiencing anger. As them to write how their nose feels when they are angry. Same with lips, eyes, hands, etc. in the end, write down 3 causes that make them angry.

How **Anger** Feels

1._____   2._____   3._____

Thinking Flexibly

Note for Kids: Hey kids! There are many ways when you think about an event or situation. There are positive, neutral, negative, and upsetting ways. You just need to recognize the negativity in you and then change it into positivity. The girl below has four clouds. Write down two positive thoughts and two negative thoughts related to an event that happened to you in past. Then decide which one is good to think about.

Mood Tracker

Note for Kids: Hello kids! Look at the bulbs in the picture. These are mood bulbs. First of all, write down different emotions in front of square boxes given at the end. Color the emotions that you have written. Then whenever you feel any emotion from the written ones, color the bulb with the color that you have given to that emotion.

Mood
Tracker

My Self-Esteem Journal

Note for Parents: It has been discovered that keeping a positive journal can aid boost sentiments of well-being and self-esteem. This self-esteem worksheet will require your kids to enter three daily items relating to their triumphs, good characteristics, and positive experiences. This worksheet is ideal for individuals who have trouble coming up with positive experiences to write about in their journals. This worksheet has been made to be as straightforward and uncomplicated as possible while still retaining critical traits for boosting self-esteem. Just complete the sentences daily with your kids to know how was their overall day. The following are some examples of prompts:

"I was delighted when..."

"Today, I was able to..."

"I did something for someone..."

Mon	Today, I was able to	
	I was delighted when	
	Something I did for someone	
Tue	I was delighted when	
	Today, I was able to	
	Something I did for someone	
Wed	I was delighted when	
	Something I did for someone	
	Today, I was able to	

Thurs	I was delighted when	
	Today, I was able to	
	Something I did for someone	
Fri	I was delighted when	
	Something I did for someone	
	Today, I was able to	
Sat	I was delighted when	
	Today, I was able to	
	Something I did for someone	
Sun	I was delighted when	
	Today, I was able to	
	Something I did for someone	

How I Handle Conflict (Questionnaire)

Note for Parents: This questionnaire is easy and quick to solve. Ask your kids to carefully read and choose the options. Help your youngster to select the real option and make them realize how their choice is wrong or right.

When there is a conflict, I;

My Response	Sometimes	Usually	Never
Complain			
Forgive			
Threaten			
Apologize			
Ignore			
Raise my Voice			
Yell			
Suggest solutions			
Walk away			
Look for a win-win			
Call someone's help			
Cry			
Upset			
Get irritated			
Use humor			
Work it out fairly			
Work towards agreement			
Make a deal			
Assign Blame			
Other:			

Anger Management Skills Card

Note for Parents: Use these colorful and engaging anger management skill cards to teach kids how to control their rage. Each of the cards features an image and a suggestion for a healthy, kid-friendly anger control method. We recommend practicing each skill at home and giving your kid a set of cards to take notes as a reminder.

This card can also be used as part of a group therapy exercise to teach kids about rage. Try putting the cards in a hat after folding them. Allow each group member to take a turn drawing a card and practicing the skill. After that, the group member can either teach the other about their expertise or exchange with another group member. Try this game if you want to try a new, interesting, and engaging rage activity for kids:

Worry Coping Cards

Talk About it

Think About What it is

Get Moving

Listen to Music

Practice a Hobby

Chapter 4: Emotion Regulation and Mindfulness

Emotion regulation is the third module of dialectical behavior therapy (DBT), and it teaches clients how to moderate negative and overpowering emotions while strengthening positive ones. This chapter has three objectives:

- Recognize one's feelings
- Lessen the emotional vulnerability
- Reduce emotional distress

Understanding that unpleasant feelings are not harmful or must be avoided is important in emotion control. They are a natural part of life, but there are ways to recognize and then let go of them, so they don't rule your kids.

Kids with high emotional sensitivity frequently go through cycles that start with an experience that prompts automatic negative thinking. These thoughts then trigger an irrational or negative emotional response, leading to self-destructive conduct. More unpleasant emotions, such as humiliation and self-loathing, follow undesirable activities.

The very first skill emphasized in DBT is mindfulness because it is nearly impossible to modify long-standing habits of feeling, thinking, and acting without mindfulness.

Mindfulness is essential for managing emotions, navigating difficult situations without escalating them, and effectively resolving interpersonal issues.

Engaging your kids' Wise Minds is another DBT basic principle that requires mindfulness as well.

The fusion of the Emotional Mind and Rational Mind is the Wise Mind. When you find your Wise Mind, you'll be able to recognize what's real or true for your kid and act on it.

Ride the Wave

Riding the wave is a mental technique in which you allow yourself to feel an emotion without reacting to it.

Consider the emotion of anger. Rather than attempting to conceal emotion, riding the wave enables your kids to notice it and choose to let it out until it naturally passes.

Note for Kids: Consider imagining a wave in the ocean. The wave represents the feeling, and all you have to do is ride it till it settles down as it reaches the beach. You can't change the wave, and you certainly can't control it. You must persevere until you reach safely.

Note for Parents: Imagery is very important when dealing with strong emotions like rage or grief. Rather than educating a kid on how to conceal emotion, riding the wave teaches them to experience it without reacting violently or dangerously. The notion of riding the wave is a crucial tool for kids to learn how to regulate and manage their emotions healthily so that their relationships do not suffer. In combination with other exercises such as radical acceptance and square breathing, riding the wave gives youngsters the tools they need to deal with more stressful and anxiety-inducing events.

Anger Thermometer

The emotions thermometer is a strategy for teaching your kids about their anger indicators and warning signals and how they alter as their emotions worsen. Before your kid can learn to manage their emotions, they must first understand their warning signs.

Label this 100-point scale with your anger symptoms, with 100 being your highest level of feelings and 0 representing no emotions (angry or depressed). On the side of the thermometer, jot down your symptoms. Thoughts, feelings, and behaviors can all be symptoms.

Emotions Thermometer

Recognizing, verbalizing, and managing feelings are vital components of a child's social development. Children as young as pre-school age can recognize their own and others' emotions, communicate their feelings, and manage their feelings. Children who demonstrate greater proficiency in these areas have stronger peer connections and are seen positively by teachers.

The Emotion Thermometers is a tool that can be used to help youngsters name their emotions and rate their severity. The colorfully painted images help kids understand each emotion, and the easy rating scales let them express how strongly they feel about each one. Thermometers can be colored to the required level, or a single mark can be made.

This material is not diagnostic, but it can be used to improve emotional literacy in various ways. Uses that have been suggested include:

- As part of a check-in procedure, use Emotion Thermometers at the start of each session.

Regularly complete this practice at the end of sessions after telling a narrative (e.g., "what were your feelings when you face this?"), or when they have an event or situation, an emotion to help children put a name to their feelings.

Explore other people's emotions to teach empathy. Use this tool to investigate how someone else might be feeling.

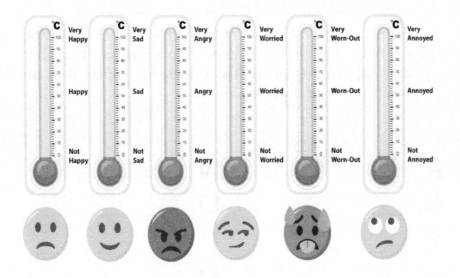

Writing my Gratitude Letter

Note for Parents: Writing a gratitude letter helps kids identify the positivity in their life and a moment to appreciate the things they have. Ask kids to write the things for which they are grateful that start with the given alphabet.

A _____   N _____

B _____   O _____

C _____   P _____

D _____   Q _____

E _____   R _____

F _____   S _____

G _____   T _____

H _____   U _____

I _____   V _____

J _____   W _____

K _____   X _____

L _____   Y _____

M _____   Z _____

Mindfulness Activities

Mindfulness is all about concentrating on the present moment and being nonjudgmental about what is happening both in and out of you. It is about paying attention to physical feelings and emotional reactions and your relationships with others and your surroundings.

1. Breathing Colors
- (5 minutes of exercise)

This activity is identical to the mindful inhaling activity, but it involves picturing colors to help your kids focus and become more aware.

- Ask kids to consider a soothing color. It can be any hue they like, as long as it conjures up images of calm.
- Assign a color to each kid that signifies tension, sadness, or rage. Whichever feelings are most relevant or appropriate to discuss with your class group.
- Kids will picture inhaling the soothing color and seeing it fill their lungs.
- Kids then picture exhaling the color representing tension, despair, or rage.

Your spoken instructions for these mindfulness activities may sound like this:

- Assume the soothing colors surround you. The air is no longer clear; instead, it has taken on a soothing color.
- Shapes can still be discerned, but your surroundings have a new color.
- As you inhale, imagine breathing in this color as well.
- Observe the color as it fills your lungs.
- Imagine that your breath is the color of stress as you exhale.

- Watch how the tension color fades into the soothing hues all around you. Keep an eye on the stress color as it fades away.
- Take a deep breath and relax.
- Take a deep breath and exhale the tension color.

2. Breathing Hands
- One hand should be spread out like a star.
- Trace the contour of your star's hand with your other hand's index finger.
- As you return to the top of your thumb, take a deep breath in.
- As you drop down through your thumbs and first finger, exhale.
- Take another deep inhale as you reach the top of your first finger.
- As you go from your first and middle fingers, exhale.
- Repeat until five slow, deep breaths have been taken.

3. Mindful Eats

(5 minutes of exercise)

For this exercise, kids will require a light snack. A fun "challenge" is often a square of chocolate, but you could instead present a piece of fruit or any other culinary item that you think will suit your kids. Take into account any allergies kids may have!

- Start by taking three deep breaths.
- Kids should take little bites or nibbles of the dish.
- Bring their attention to the eating experiences. Ask them questions.
    - Can you describe the flavor? Is it savory or sweet?

- How does it feel on your tongue when you eat it?
- Do you have to smash it between your jaws, or can it dissolve slowly in your mouth?
- Experiment with taking a smaller or larger bite.
- How does this alter the experience of eating this food?
- As you swallow the food, pay attention to which parts of your mouth, jaw, and body move.
- Take a moment between bites to note any changes in your mouth or body feelings.

4. Observe your Ability to be Mindful

For Kids: Hear the sounds around you without adding any comments, just noticing what you hear.

- Keep an eye on your breathing.
- Observe how you feel when you inhale and exhale, paying attention to how your tummy rises and falls as you breathe.
- Sit on a bench outside and watch what happens in front of your eyes without turning your head or identifying what you see.
- The Observing skill can make you feel alive in the present moment, rather than lost in the past or looking forward to the future.

Good-Bye Letter to Grief

Most adults find it difficult to speak openly about dying. Words like "dead" and "died" are softened and renamed "passed on" and "no longer with us." Too much talk about mortality or asking too several questions is frowned upon.

The subject of death can be even more emotional for children. However, evidence indicates that shielding children from reality may be counterproductive. Talking to kids about mortality in code and metaphor, or as if it is a question that needs to be swiftly addressed and dismissed, just confuses them.

The Children Grief: Recommendations for worksheet contains concise research-based recommendations for talking to children about the death of a loved one and assisting them in coping with it.

This handout is for parents and caregivers who are unsure how to handle this difficult topic or want some reassurance. Therapy can be used to rehearse these talks or to identify and solve problems with difficult-to-implement recommendations.

My Good-Bye Letter to Grief

To: _____

I am saying good-bye beacuse _____
_____

Saying good-bye makes me feel _____

I remeber a time when we _____
_____

You taught me _____

Something, I want you to know is _____
_____

I will always remember _____

From: _____

My Behavior Chart

Note for Parents: Using the Behavior Chart worksheet, support your kids to attain their objectives. This worksheet can help kids stay on track with various goals by keeping track of when they are completed or not. Your kids can hold themselves accountable for personal goals like exercising, eating healthy, and finishing homework by keeping track of their consistency.

Behavior charts can be quite useful when dealing with a parent who wants to increase their child's chore compliance. When their children have finished a duty, parents might use stickers or other markers to let them know. This strategy works nicely in conjunction with a well-implemented bonus system!

Fill out this behavior chart with your kids.

My Behavior Chart

	Monday	Tuesday	Wednesday	Thursday	Friday
I listened to my teacher	😐	😐	😐	😐	😐
I followed directions	😐	😐	😐	😐	😐
I was kind to other kids	😐	😐	😐	😐	😐
I acomplished my goals	😐	😐	😐	😐	😐
I played with kids	😐	😐	😐	😐	😐

Comments _____

_____

Note for Kids: For this activity, set a weekly goal and mark the days you worked on the goal and how much the effort is done.

Goals	Mon	Tues	Wed	Thurs	Fri	Sat	Sun

Emotion Regulation Worksheet

Individuals are taught to employ skills in transformation and acceptance in Dialectical Behavioral Therapy (DBT). Emotion control skills are classified as "change" skills. DBT emotion regulation skills, as the name implies, assist the individuals in learning to moderate their feelings to better cope with their current situation.

Note: This DBT worksheet covers emotional regulation skills such as opposite action, checking facts, P.L.E.A.S.E., and concentrating on positive events. This worksheet can be used as a teaching tool or a take-home recall for patients practicing DBT techniques.

Consider the following questions:

What happened to make me feel this way?

What assumptions do I have about the situation?

Do my feelings and thoughts correspond to the reality of the situation?

My Safety Crisis Plan

Note for Kids: Identify your triggering signs and use your coping strategies to keep yourself safe and your emotions in control. Consider answering the following questions:

- **Triggers and Stressors**

Behaviors and Emotions that put you at emotional risk:

_____

_____

_____

_____

_____

_____

_____

_____

- **Warning Signs**

Your behaviors that show you are more indulging in negativity:

_____

_____

_____

_____

_____

_____

_____

_____

- **Things to Do**

My goals for healthy behavior:

_____

_____

_____

_____

_____

_____

_____

_____

- **Coping Skills**

Strategies I use to deal with my negative behavior:

_____

_____

_____

_____

_____

_____

_____

_____

- **My Reminders**

Things I need to remember:

_____

_____

_____

_____

_____

_____

_____

_____

Trust, Faith, Love

Note for Kids: Hey Kids! Trust, Faith, and Love are three important things in life. These three things make a healthy family and a stronger bond with family members. Consider this house your happy home. Label the windows, door, grass, tree, and everything with the words that come to your mind when you think of a happy home with Trust, Faith, and Love. For example, I will label the window "a window to let go of negativity and appreciate the happiness in home".

Earn it Back

Note for Kids: We all abandoned many things and many are lost due to our negligence, carelessness, or sometimes our rude behaviors. It is time to recall all those things and earn them back. Answer the following questions and work on yourself to earn those things back into your life.

Earning Back my Privileges

Because of these behaviors, (Write behaviors)

_____

_____

_____

_____

I have lost the privileges of

_____

_____

_____

_____

My behaviors were wrong because

_____

_____

_____

_____

To earn these privileges back, I have to

_____

_____

_____

_____

Once I do these things, I will be able to earn back my privileges.

_____

_____

_____

_____

__

My Signature

Happy Place

Note for Kids: Recognize your happy place. Think of the things, events, or circumstances that make you feel happy and write them down in the thinking clouds.

Balloon Breathing

Balloon breathing is a mindfulness activity to help kids relax whenever they are struggling with emotions. Ask kids to follow the directions below.

To quiet your mind and body, combine deep breathing and motion in this technique. Show your youngster how to do it and have them copy you.

*You have the **OPTION** of sitting or standing.

~Make a fist and place it on the forehead.
~Begin by slowly inhaling and exhaling.
~Lift your arms overhead as you inhale, as if you were filling up a balloon.
~Your hands should look like a large, spherical balloon on your forehead when your chests are full of air.

~Slowly move your hands to your head as you breathe.
~Match the time of your inhalation with lifting your arms and match your exhalation time with lowering your arms.
~Try to lengthen your breathing with each inhale as much as you can.
Repeat the breath and arm motion 2-4 times further.
~On your last breath, push your jaws together and push out the air.

Square Breathing

Among the most basic DBT techniques, square breathing is also one of the most successful techniques. Square breathing is a stress and anxiety-relieving guided breathing practice that anyone may do.

The following is how it works:

- Count to four as you inhale.
- Hold your breath for four counts.
- To a count of four, exhale.
- Hold it for four counts again.

When a person is upset or overwhelmed, square breath is a simple and efficient technique for calming down. Teaching to take a breath in a highly emotional situation is crucial for stress management and maintaining positive relationships because it allows the participant to calm down before reacting.

If you are working with younger kids, another way to teach this method is to have them blow slowly into a pretend bubble.

Parents place their fingers in front of their children's faces, palms closed, as if praying. The child is then asked to "blow a bubble." This is done by imagining bubbles with your hands. As your youngster blows into the bubbles, spread your hands slightly wider as the size of the bubble grows. The bigger the bubble develops, the slower and harder your child blows. Keep growing the bubble, although not as much, if they take small, quick breaths.

As the youngster appears to relax, increase the bubble size in your hands till you can tell that your child is at ease. Ask your youngster to burst the bubble and blow away once you are sure he or she is calm.

This is a simple approach to introducing controlled breathing to your child at an early age while also distracting them from whatever is bothering them. It also allows you to teach your child a crucial skill at a young age and offers impatient parents a few minutes to catch their breath.

Flower Breathing

Instructions for Kids: Choose a comfortable upright standing or sitting position, such as sitting down, cross-legged, or on your heels. If it is easier for you, close your eyes and focus on the sounds of your breath. Assume you are holding a flower in your hand. Consider the flower's hue and scent. After that, take a big inhale and pretend to smell the bloom. Then exhale and act as if you are blowing flower petals. If feasible, repeat the cycle of a powerful inhale and a calm exhale for a few minutes. Each time you inhale, you may imagine smelling a new bloom. You may perhaps picture yourself seated in a flower-filled meadow.

This floral breath is a simple approach to help kids become more conscious of breathing. You might even act as though you are smelling hot chocolate and then blow it away to cool it down. You might pretend to smell the autumn air (inhale) and then scatter leaves during the autumn season (exhale).

Positive Self-Talk Flower

Note for Kids: Talking to yourself is an excellent way to bring positivity to life. I have a flower for you. Talk positively to yourself in the mirror and write down the appreciation sentences that you told yourself. Here is an example for you.

Now it is your turn:

Chapter 5: Walking the Middle Path: DBT Skills for Parents

Dialectical Behavioral Therapy, or DBT, is a type of therapy aimed at assisting persons experiencing behavioral difficulties due to trauma. DBT has four major goals that have been shown to assist young people in rethinking their behavior and managing stress.

When children have access to stressful experiences or childhood trauma, such as dealing with someone who has a mental illness, exposure to domestic violence, or enduring physical or emotional maltreatment, their brains and bodies react differently to stress and conflict.

Young people from such environments are more prone to suffer from anxiety, sadness, angry outbursts, and trouble sustaining healthy interpersonal connections.

To help these young people, Ranch employs Dialectical Behavioral Therapy (DBT). DBT is a skills-based strategy that has been utilized since the 1980s and is evidence-based. In this chapter, you will learn some crucial skills that are necessary for parents to learn when their kids are suffering from mental health issues to help them handle emotions.

Riding the wave, failing forward, moment to pause, etc. are among the skills we discuss. Continue reading to find out more. Taking the Mid Path is a collection of dialectical behavior therapy (DBT) skills for parents. These skills help in better communication between parents and kids, allowing them to retain a bond during this trying time. Discover what this skill is, how to use it at home, and how it can assist your family in mastering it.

Failing Forward

For most parents, failing forward is challenging to master because it entails using our failures as a springboard for growth and learning.

As a culture, we have a propensity to focus solely on achievement. Failure is often viewed as something to be embarrassed by or avoided, but failing forward is about embracing our setbacks and using them to propel us ahead. This is a very crucial ability for parents.

Allowing your child to accept the logical consequences of his or her choices is what failing forward entails for parents. You let your child take a lesser mark for not turning in their homework on time rather than bringing it to school if they forgot their assignment because they were not organized or couldn't prepare the night before. That "failure" will give them the internal desire to be more prepared the next time.

Instead of chastising your kid for not being organized, you may inquire about their experience of not having their schoolwork ready and how they thought about the lower grade. Parents may say that the internal sensation of struggle will motivate you to be better organized next time. It also allows young people to learn from experience, which will benefit them in the long run.

By praising failure as a chance for growth, failing forward removes the fear of failure. It is a good technique to help kids cope with stress and anxiety. It removes expectations from most circumstances and teaches your child that failure does not imply they have failed as a person and that there's always room for improvement.

Communicate Understanding

When speaking to your child, make it clear that you appreciate where he is coming from.

"It makes sense why you are hurting and upset," says your kid. "I'm sure this is a frustrating scenario."

"I get where you are coming from, but here is why you are wrong," you can say.

Suppose you cannot find a way to justify your kid's actions; look for their emotions, which are always valid. While kids may make poor decisions when upset, anger is an acceptable emotion for them to experience. Accept them and their emotions and help them deal with the scenarios in a comforting way through effective communication.

Recognizing your Own Emotions

When dealing with powerful emotions, it is challenging to validate your kid genuinely. Self-care is important, the same as being mindful of your feelings. Walking the Middle Path requires both parties to take a step back from their own emotions to see the other person's point of view. When you are aware of your current feelings, you can take a conscious step back to see things from your kid's point of view.

Using Past Experiences

Consider what your kid has had to go through and how those events may be affecting his feelings when affirming him, especially if you are having trouble understanding where he is coming from. He may be reacting this way because he has been bullied in the past or had a traumatic event when he was younger. You can help him see an alternative way of doing things once you have indicated that you know what he is going through.

Increasing Positive Behaviors

The easiest solution is not always the best option. "Catch" your child doing something positive and compliment her on a behavior you want her to continue. You are probably not pleased anymore that she follows simple rules like placing her dish in the washer, drying her towel after a bath, and putting her hairdryer away now that she is no longer a toddler. As a parent of kids, it is all too tempting to get caught up in the behaviors she has to change. Make an effort to compliment your daughter on her good qualities, even if they seem insignificant. She will be more likely to do it again when you tell her that you have noticed and appreciated anything she has done. Do the same with your son.

Offering an incentive (a good outcome) as soon as feasible is another way to encourage excellent conduct. Perhaps she/he receives an extra 15 minutes that night or is freed of a duty. Even spending quality time with you might be a rewarding experience. You may offer to go on a drive with her/him, get your dressing done together, or play the game with her/him. This will encourage kids to engage in more beneficial activities in the future.

Some kids may choose praise and recognition above a reward, while others prefer the opposite. When intrinsic motivation is low during this phase, one of these strategies is sufficient to inspire your kids to continue participating in beneficial activities.

Decreasing Unhealthy Behaviors

One of the most difficult aspects of parenthood is attempting to change or stop your child's bad behavior. You would like your youngster to stop shouting, doing drugs, self-harming, or staying up late. Most parents' first reaction is to escalate punishment by grounding their kids, taking away their phones, or taking away their car keys. This lets your kids know they have done something wrong, but it does not always help them change their ways. Natural and values-based consequences are the two sorts of consequences you need to focus on to change unhealthy behaviors.

Riding Out the Extinction Burst

Imagine your kid is learning, as most kids do, that the most efficient way to get you to say yes is to throw a tantrum in public. What happens if you keep saying no one day after another? She intensifies her tantrum. You must have ignored this the first time it happened. A public scream always works, so it would not have been loud enough. The tantrum gets bigger, louder, and snottier as you keep your position. From a psychological standpoint, she understands that this is the most guaranteed manner of obtaining the cinnamon candy she despises yet desperately requires. As a result, she will keep trying until either you or she quits up. The last alternative, on the other hand, may take some time. This is mass extinction. It is a temporary increase in the behavior you are attempting to stop to achieve the desired outcome she used to get from it. Please remember that your daughter may not be escalating on purpose.

Unfortunately, these outbursts do not stop when you are a toddler. You might expect your kid daughter's behavior to worsen before she gives up when you are trying to improve it. You will almost certainly have to go through several unpleasant events, some of which may continue longer than you expect. It is far easier to give in to the behavior when you have been worn down, but doing so will merely reinforce that the issue behavior is still effective. So, if you are determined to assist your daughter in changing a behavior, be ready to ride out the extinction burst. You are aware of what is going on, and you are more determined than your adolescent — even if she is the most obstinate. Do not be afraid to enhance your self-care and brush up on your distress tolerance abilities to get through this difficult moment.

Values-Based Consequences

It is not always possible to sit back and let your daughter suffer the natural repercussions of her behavior. The natural result of self-harming behavior, substance misuse, and disordered eating (to mention a few) might be death. When it is necessary to intervene in your daughter's behavior, we advocate using a values-based consequence.

Families and individuals have values, whether they've been defined or not. Kindness, respect, hygiene, security, openness, and love are common family values. You would engage with the value of security if your daughter participated in self-harming activities. Her values-based consequence could be hospitalization or residential treatment to keep her safe. Values-based repercussions, of course, do not have to be reserved for severe situations. For instance, your daughter may taunt her younger brother till he sobs. She does not follow in her family's footsteps of kindness. As a result, you may ask her to perform one good deed for her brother a day next week. Make your repercussions as quick, values-based, imaginative, and directly tied to the behavior you are attempting to change as possible.

The Message to Remember

There will be a lot of reminders for parents who are teaching DBT skills to their children. It is also critical for families to model this conduct and to be patient with their children as they learn. When families encounter situations that they could have managed better, it is a good idea to ask the kids how the issue could have been handled better and what they (and parents) will try to make it better next time (once everyone is calm). Parents can offer their children an emotional vocabulary and skillset by recognizing and naming the abilities they need to sustain good relationships, manage emotions, practice mindfulness, and endure stress by identifying and naming the skills.

It will take a lot of practice and focused dialogues for parents to teach their children any form of resilience or relationship skills. It is acceptable to inform your children that you are attempting to teach them a specific ability. This will help children understand that their behavior and emotions are under their control, and they can still choose how they react to them. Ask in the comment section on *Amazon* if you have any concerns or would like more info about how DBT or any other proven therapies might be able to help your family.

Made in the USA
Monee, IL
30 May 2023

34965341R00066